FIESTA!

ITALY

GROLIER EDUCATIONAL
SHERMAN TURNPIKE, DANBURY, CONNECTICUT 06816

Published for Grolier Educational
Sherman Turnpike, Danbury, Connecticut
by Marshall Cavendish Books
an imprint of Times Editions Pte Ltd
Times Centre, 1 New Industrial Road, Singapore 536196
Tel: (65) 2848844 Fax: (65) 2854871
Email: te@corp.tpl.com.sg
World Wide Web:
http://www.timesone.com.sg/te

Set ISBN: 0-7172-9099-9
Volume ISBN: 0-7172-9101-4

Library of Congress Cataloging-in-Publication Data
Italy.
p.cm. -- (Fiesta!)
Includes index.
Summary: Describes the customs and beliefs connected to some of the special occasions celebrated in Italy,
including Christmas and Easter, Raduno, Fiesta dei Morti, and the Olive Festival.
Includes recipes and related activities.
ISBN 0-7172-9101-4
1. Festivals -- Italy -- Juvenile literature. 2. Italy -- Social life and customs -- Juvenile literature. [1. Festivals -- Italy.
2. Holidays -- Italy. 3. Italy -- Social life and customs.]
I. Grolier Educational (Firm) II. Series: Fiesta! (Danbury, Conn.)
GT4852.A2173 1997
394.26945--dc21
97-18672
CIP
AC

Marshall Cavendish Books Editorial Staff
Editorial Director: Ellen Dupont
Series Designer: Joyce Mason
Crafts devised and created by Susan Moxley
Music arrangements by Harry Boteler
Photographs by Bruce Mackie
Subeditors: Susan Janes, Judy Fovargue
Production: Craig Chubb

For this volume
Editor: Tessa Paul
Writer: Tim Cooke
Designer: Trevor Vertigan
Consultant: Emily Stefania Coscione
Editorial Assistant: Lorien Kite

Printed in Italy

Adult supervision advised for all crafts and recipes
particularly those involving sharp instruments and heat.

CONTENTS

ITALY:

On the southern edge of Europe, Italy is shaped like a long boot. Its toe points to the island of Sicily.

Switzerland

Oglio

Ticino

Turin

Milan

Tanaro

France

Genoa

Monaco

▲ **Christian images**, like this carving of Jesus in the arms of His mother Mary, are popular in Italy. Most Italians are Roman Catholics.

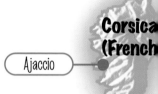

Corsica (French)

Ajaccio

Sardinia (Italian)

◀ **Tuscany** is a hilly area in the north of Italy. Fine wines and olive oils are made on Tuscan country estates. The towns of Siena and Florence are attractions of the area.

Cagliari

Mediterranean Sea

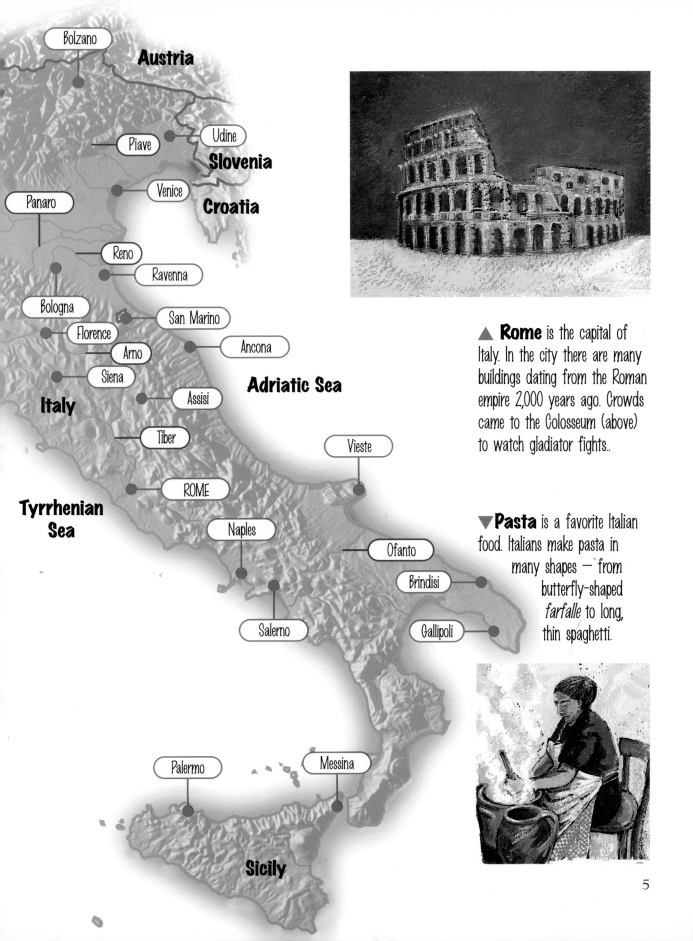

Bolzano

Austria

Piave

Udine

Slovenia

Venice

Croatia

Panaro

Reno

Ravenna

Bologna

San Marino

Florence

Ancona

Arno

Siena

Adriatic Sea

Assisi

Italy

Tiber

Vieste

ROME

Tyrrhenian Sea

Naples

Ofanto

Brindisi

Salerno

Gallipoli

Palermo

Messina

Sicily

▲ **Rome** is the capital of Italy. In the city there are many buildings dating from the Roman empire 2,000 years ago. Crowds came to the Colosseum (above) to watch gladiator fights..

▼**Pasta** is a favorite Italian food. Italians make pasta in many shapes — from butterfly-shaped *farfalle* to long, thin spaghetti.

5

RELIGIONS

Italy is a Christian country, and most Italian Christians are Roman Catholics. Many Italian holidays celebrate Catholic festivals.

CHRISTIANS believe that Jesus Christ was the son of God who came to Earth around 2,000 years ago. He died after he was "crucified" – nailed to a wooden cross. But three days later, they say, he came back to life.

Christians say that before Jesus died He chose Peter, one of his followers, to be leader of all Christians. They believe that today the Pope, who is the head of the Catholic Church, is doing the same job that Peter did. Catholics say that God chooses each Pope to lead the Church. The Pope tells Catholics how to behave well.

The Pope lives in the Vatican, a small area within Italy's capital city, Rome. The Vatican is in fact a separate country from Italy. It has its own banks and government. But people still think of Italy as the home of Catholicism.

Catholics like to have religious pictures and carvings around them.

Catholics honor Mary, the mother of Jesus. She is special because God chose her to give birth to Jesus.

They keep images of Jesus, of Mary, Jesus's mother, and of the saints. The saints are people who lived according to God's laws. They are made saints by the Pope long after they have died.

Catholics believe that saints are close to God and can pass people's prayers on to Him. Many Catholic children are named after saints. Villages, towns, and even some countries have a patron saint who watches over them. The patron saint of Italy is Saint Francis.

The Catholic Church is very rich and powerful. For hundreds of years rich Christians left money and land to the Church when they died. The Church paid for many beautiful works of art. Churches in Italy are full of them. Until the 1400s Catholicism was the main form of Christianity. In the 1500s a German monk named Martin Luther started a protest against the Catholic Church. He said the Church had lost touch with God. Luther's protest led to a new form of Christianity, Protestantism. There are now Protestants all over the world.

GREETINGS FROM **ITALY!**

Many important things have happened in Italy. Rome, the country's capital, was the center of the great Roman Empire 2,000 years ago. You can still see the remains of buildings and works of art from that time. In the period 1400–1700 many great artists worked in Italy. Today tourists come to cities like Venice, Florence, and Rome to see their works. Most people speak Italian. In the north of the country near the border with France, Austria, and Switzerland many speak French and German as well as Italian.

How do you say...

Hello

Buongiorno

Goodbye

Ciao

Thank you

Grazie

Peace

Pace

CHRISTMAS

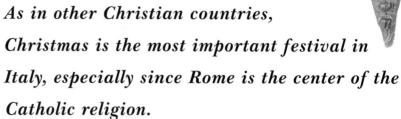

As in other Christian countries, Christmas is the most important festival in Italy, especially since Rome is the center of the Catholic religion.

The head of the Catholic Church, the Pope, lives in the Vatican in Rome. Pilgrims from Italy and abroad visit for his Christmas sermon.

In their homes people decorate their Christmas trees with balls and boxes of nougat. Each home has a nativity scene, or model of Christ's birthplace. The nativity scene, or *presepio*, first came from Italy.

On Christmas Day children receive gifts from Babbo Natale, or Father Christmas. But there is another day for presents, Epiphany.

This day, January 6, celebrates the visit of the three kings to the baby Jesus. Epiphany presents come from *La Befana*. She is old and looks like a witch. She walks over the rooftops with a sack of toys and treats to give to children. But if they have been bad, she leaves coal and ash.

No one eats meat on Christmas Eve. But on Christmas Day itself families sit down to a roast meat meal.

NATIVITY SCENE

YOU WILL NEED
2 cups flour
2 cups salt
1 tbsp oil
Water
Garlic press
Baking tray
Water-based paints
Cardboard

The Nativity is a scene showing the birth of Christ. It includes figures of the baby Jesus, Mary, Joseph, the three wise men, and even the animals who were in the barn where Jesus was born. They are all a part of the Christmas story.

1 Make the dough by mixing the flour, salt, and oil. Add enough water so that it makes a firm dough. Knead with your hands for five minutes. Roll out the dough on a floured surface, and cut out the shapes of the figures you want to make.

2 To make the hair, put the dough through a garlic press. Lay out the figures on a baking tray. Get an adult to help you with the oven. Bake the figures in a cool oven for 3 to 4 hours until the dough is hard to the touch. Let them cool, then paint and decorate them. Glue a folded strip of cardboard onto the back to make them stand up.

THE NATIVITY STORY

Every Christmas the story of the birth of Jesus is told. Children act out the events in their classrooms. Everywhere there are models of the stable, with the baby in the manger, His mother Mary and her husband, the shepherds, the kings, and the farm animals.

JOSEPH STOOD outside his carpenter's shop. He thought about his wife Mary. The Angel Gabriel had come down from heaven and given Mary a special message. She was to be the Mother of the Son of God. Joseph was worried because the baby was soon to be born, but Joseph had to travel a long distance.

The Roman Emperor had ordered that everyone return to the town of their birth. He wanted to take a census. This order meant that Joseph and Mary had to go to Bethlehem where he had been born. Joseph found a donkey for Mary to ride while he walked.

For three days and three nights Joseph and Mary traveled, until at last they reached the gates of Bethlehem.

They stopped at the first inn they saw, but when Joseph asked for a room, the innkeeper replied that there were none left. Joseph tried every other inn in the town, but the message was always the same: "No room at the inn." At last an innkeeper told them of a stable they could sleep in.

They rushed there just in time for Mary to give birth to the baby Jesus. She laid Him in a manger filled with hay. The animals moved closer to gaze at the new-born babe. Mary and Joseph felt happier than they had ever felt before. It was clear now that God had intended His Son to be born in a stable.

Some shepherds with a little boy crept shyly into the stable. They knelt

at the manger. The boy brought a lamb as a present. They told Mary the Angel Gabriel appeared before them and told them a king was born in Bethlehem. Then three kings, wise men from far away, stepped into the stable. They had journeyed from the east, they said, following a brilliant star that finally stopped above the stable. The kings bowed their heads before the baby.

All in that humble stable knew the Son of God had been born.

CARNEVALE

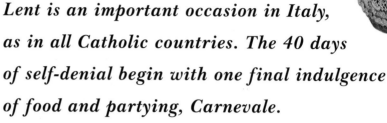

Lent is an important occasion in Italy, as in all Catholic countries. The 40 days of self-denial begin with one final indulgence of food and partying, Carnevale.

Lent begins on Ash Wednesday, 40 days before Easter. It marks the time spent in the wilderness when Jesus resisted the temptations of the devil. Traditionally, Catholics ate no meat during Lent. Today people often give up something they really like, such as chocolate. But everyone looks forward to Lent because it begins with *Carnevale*.

Every Italian town and village has its own Carnevale. The word means "goodbye to meat." It was the time when everyone ate up all the food that might go bad in the next 40 days.

The oldest and most famous of all the Italian carnivals is in Venice. The city is full of canals, and people are rowed around in boats called *gondolas*.

At Carnevale the city of Venice comes alive. People wear historical costumes and masks, and parade through the narrow streets. Balls go on all night for people lucky enough to be invited. But anyone can put on a mask and join the fun in the streets.

Arlecchino, a clown from traditional Italian drama, is a common choice for costumes during the Carnevale in Venice.

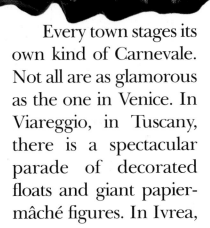

The masks the Venetians wear during Carnevale are highly elaborate and are often based on historical designs.

in the north of Italy, the people reenact an old revolt when the townspeople overthrew their ruler. They hurl thousands of oranges at each other, until everyone is covered in juice. Then, bruised and tired, they all gather in the town square for a feast of *La Fagiolata*. This rich and tasty bean stew is the last indulgence before Lent.

Every town stages its own kind of Carnevale. Not all are as glamorous as the one in Venice. In Viareggio, in Tuscany, there is a spectacular parade of decorated floats and giant papier-mâché figures. In Ivrea,

Wherever people celebrate Carnevale, it is a time for jokes and pranks. The Italians say that at Carnevale "anything goes." They set off firecrackers, throw streamers, and play games such as climbing a greasy pole.

After the parade, however, everything is quickly quiet again. Carnival is over for another year. Now it is time for Lent.

Venice is famous for its beautiful glassware. This gondola is blown from glass.

EASTER

Easter is one of the most important festivals in the Christian year. Traditionally it is marked throughout Italy by church services and processions that go on throughout Holy Week.

Easter in Italy, as in all Christian countries, is an important festival. It marks the time of Christ's crucifixion and of his rising from the dead. But although Easter is a religious occasion, it is also a time to celebrate the coming spring. Flowers begin to bloom; new fruits and vegetables appear on every table.

Festivals go on throughout Italy in Holy Week, which leads up to Good Friday, the day of the crucifixion. On that day people on the tiny island of Procida carry a statue of the Virgin Mary through the streets.

On Easter Sunday, the day Jesus rose from the dead, the villagers in Sulmona enact a meeting between Mary and Jesus after the resurrection. Florence, in Tuscany, stages a spectacular fireworks display in front of the cathedral. For many people the highlight of Easter is the Pope's address to the crowds in Rome.

Easter is the end of Lent. After self-denial it is time to indulge again. Easter foods include lamb, eggs, and wheat. Lamb is a symbol of Christ and the spring. Eggs, either chocolate or

Traditional Easter food includes cakes and breads enriched with fruit and nuts, and often baked in symbolic shapes, such as that of a dove.

Painted eggs and tiny chicks are a common symbol of new life and springtime.

of candies and cakes. There are chocolate eggs and lambs, and cakes shaped like doves, which symbolize peace.

Easter Monday is a good time to picnic. The whole family goes out to the countryside and enjoys the warm spring air.

real, are a sign of life; and wheat is a symbol of resurrection.

Easter is a time for enjoying plenty

THE CRUCIFIXION

The story of Christ's death and resurrection are at the heart of the Christian faith. Christians believe that Christ sacrificed Himself to save mankind. Then, by rising from the dead, He showed that God offers eternal life. Crucifixion was a slow, painful death. By allowing Himself to be killed in this way, Jesus accepted a great deal of suffering.

The figure of Jesus on the cross is often seen in Catholic churches. It is a powerful reminder of the agony Christ endured.

Jesus had to carry His own cross to the crucifixion. In some Italian towns this journey is acted out on Good Friday. A man playing Jesus carries the heavy cross through the streets.

RADUNO

At the end of May the town of Taormina on the island of Sicily celebrates an ancient victory with displays of traditional puppets and carts.

In the last three days of May the Sicilians mark a great victory won by the 9th-century emperor Charlemagne over the Moors, or Muslims.

Decorated carts parade in the streets. The cart was the peasants' usual way to travel and an important possession. But the main part of the festival are special shows of "*i pupi,*" or traditional puppets.

Sicilian peasants traditionally decorate their carts and animals.

CHARLEMAGNE

Charlemagne lived from around 742 to 814. He was king of a people called the Franks who lived in what is today France.

Charlemagne was a Christian. He led his armies against non-Christians, such as the Saxon peoples, and forced them to adopt the faith. He also defeated the Moors of northern Africa, who ruled Spain at that time. As a reward for his deeds the Pope crowned Charlemagne Holy Roman Emperor. His kingdom, called the Holy Roman Empire, covered most of western Europe. Charlemagne did much to help establish Christianity in Europe. He became a popular hero.

Many legends and myths grew up around him and the valor of his brave knights, who were called *paladins*.

In Sicily puppet theaters have been popular for 400 years. The wooden puppets are moved by strings. They act out stories about the knights of the Middle Ages. The deeds of Charlemagne and his knights are a great favorite.

The shows are very lively. The puppeteer speaks all the voices, while the audience shouts at the villains and cheers the heroes. The armor and swords of the puppets clank as they fight noisy duels. The knights endure many difficult trials. But at the end of the story they always emerge victorious.

The puppets' arms are specially jointed so that they can act out spectacular and noisy fights with their swords.

17

PALIO

In the medieval hill town of Siena exciting horse races keep alive the city's history by recalling the color, noise, and splendor of Italy during the 15th century.

Twice each year the people of Siena in Tuscany stage a colorful and dangerous horse race. The race is run on July 2 and on August 16. Its name, *Palio,* comes from the Italian word for the banner given to the winner.

The Palio is over 500 years old. A long time ago the different neighborhoods of the town, called *contrade,* began sports contests. The old games used fighting skills, such as riding, fencing, and archery. Today the 17 contrade only compete in riding. But the event still arouses lots of pride in each of the local communities.

The race takes place in the town square, or *campo.* Race day is colorful and noisy. The narrow streets echo with the drums and trumpets. The men wear costumes from the 15th century. Each contrada has its own bright flag.

Before the race begins, a procession of

MAKE A FLAG

YOU WILL NEED
Thin cotton fabric
A wooden pole or stick
Fabric paints
Colored ribbon
White paper

1 Draw the flag design on the paper. Stretch the fabric over the paper so the design shows through. Trace the design onto the fabric. Leave a margin on one side to wrap around the pole.

2 Paint in the design on the flag with the fabric paints. When it's dry, get an adult to iron the flag. Sew or glue one side of the flag to make a pocket for the pole to slip through. To decorate the pole, wrap the colored ribbons around it. Tie the ribbon in a bow to secure it on to the pole.

musicians, page-boys, and jockeys enters the square. Flag-wavers twirl and throw the flags of the contrade in the air.

The horses race three times around the square at a furious pace. After the hours of waiting the race is over in 75 seconds. The winner receives the palio, which always has an image of the Virgin Mary on it. His contrada will keep it until the next time.

Siena's most famous dish is panforte, a deliciously sweet cake made of honey, dried fruits, nuts, and spices.

FERRAGOSTO

As the August sun beats down, everyone looks forward to Ferragosto. This festival, dedicated to the Virgin Mary, is also a time to take a break from work, eat and drink, and escape from the baking towns and cities.

The hottest month in Italy is August. Many shops and offices are closed. Many people take their vacations. But Ferragosto, which falls on August 15, is a holiday for everyone.

The Ferragosto festival is dedicated to the Virgin Mary, but it has its roots in the pagan religion of ancient Rome. The word itself comes from the Latin phrase

Many Ferragosto celebrations include this ice-cream dessert from Sicily, called a bombe.

THE VIRGIN MARY

Mary, the mother of Jesus, is very important for Catholics. They worship her and dedicate churches to her. For them she is a symbol of purity because she gave birth to Jesus when she was still a virgin.

Mary, who is sometimes called the Madonna, is also an ideal mother. She is popular in societies where the family is important. In this statue the Angel Gabriel tells Mary that she will have a child, Jesus.

for the festival of the Roman emperor Augustus, for whom the month was named. The Romans celebrated their festival on August 1. But Christians moved it to August 15 because that was the day that the Virgin Mary was said to have ascended to heaven.

Ferragosto is still both a religious and a nonreligious, or secular, holiday. The Virgin Mary is very important to Catholics, and many churches are dedicated to her. Whole villages and towns turn out to see statues of her being carried through the streets and blessed by the priest.

After everyone has paid respects

MOZZARELLA & TOMATO SALAD

SERVES 4 TO 6

4 large tomatoes
½ pound mozzarella cheese, drained
Fresh basil leaves
Ripe olives
Salt and pepper
2 tbsp olive oil

1 Ask an adult to thinly slice tomatoes and mozzarella cheese.
2 Tear some basil leaves into tiny pieces. Leave small sprigs whole.
3 Arrange tomatoes and cheese on platter; add basil and olives on top. Add salt and pepper. Drizzle olive oil over top. Serve.

to the Virgin, it is time for the secular part of the day. Everyone gets together to feast.

Many people head for the beach or out into the country for a

picnic. Or perhaps they visit a restaurant to try the local food. Whatever they do, this is a chance to forget work and enjoy the sunshine. Tomorrow will come soon enough.

A prominent feature of this pottery model of Italy's fruits are the grapes that produce the country's famous wine. Vineyards cover much of the central Italian hills.

SAINT FRANCIS

On October 4 celebrations of the life of Saint Francis are concentrated in Assisi, the historic town where he was born, where he preached, and where he died.

Saint Francis is Italy's patron saint. That means he is believed to take special care of Italy and of the Italians. They know him as San Francesco.

On his Saint's Day, October 4, there are celebrations all over the country, but thousands of Italians travel to Assisi for the occasion.

· This city is built on a hill. At the foot of the hill is Saint Mary of the Angels, a very old, tiny chapel which is now contained within a huge basilica.

Boys and men dress in robes such as priests usually wear. The robes are in the colors of their town or neighborhood. They are part of a procession from the town to the church. Many of the groups carry an effigy of Saint Francis on their shoulders.

At the head of the grand procession is a Franciscan monk. He carries doves on each of his outstretched arms. Often he walks barefoot. He does this in memory of Francis, who chose a life of poverty, and who was so gentle even the

birds stopped to listen to his sweet voice.

In the basilica and in the tiny chapel prayers are said for the Saint.

Shops and offices are closed, but street stalls sell food and toys. Francis is a much-loved saint, and his day is a joyous day.

A SAINT FRANCIS PRAYER

Laudato si, mi Signore, con tucte
  le tue creature,
specialmente messor lo frate sole,
lo quale jorna, at illumini per lui;
et ellu è bellu e radiante
  cum grande splendore;
de Te, Altissimu, porta significatione.

Laudato si, mi Signore,
  per sora luna e le stelle;
in celu l'ài formate clarite et
  pretiose et belle.

Laudato si, mi Signore, per frate vento
et per aere et nubilo et sereno
  et onne tempo,
per le quali alle tue creature
  dai sostentamento.
Laudato si, mi Signore, per frate focu,
  per lo quale ennallumini la nocte,
et ello è bellu, et jocundo, et robustoso,
et forte.
Laudato si, mi Signore, per sora
nostra madre terra,
la quale ne sustenta e governa,
e produce diversi fructi, con coloriti
fiori et herba.

Praised be You, my Lord, with all your creatures, especially Sir Brother Sun, who is the day and through whom you give us light. And he is beautiful and radiant with splendor and bears likeness of You, Most High One.

Praised be You, my Lord, through Sister Moon and the stars in heaven: You formed them clear and precious and beautiful.

Praised be You, my Lord, through brother Wind and through the air, cloudy and serene, and every kind of weather, you sustain your creatures.

Praised be You, my Lord, through Brother Fire, through whom You light the night, and he is beautiful and playful and robust and strong.
Praised be You, my Lord, through our sister Mother Earth, who sustains us, governs us, and who produces varied fruits with colored flowers and herbs.

Saint Francis of Assisi was famous not only for his humble life of poverty but for his writing. His poems and prayers are read and loved by modern Catholics. This prayer is taken from a larger work known as "The Canticle of Brother Sun."

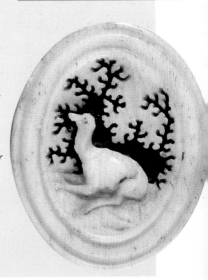

23

THE STORY OF SAINT FRANCIS

Francis of Assisi was the founder of a great order of monks, men who live in communities and serve God. During his lifetime many stories were told of the goodness of Francis. Even the birds and flowers responded to his gentle ways.

WHEN FRANCIS WAS BORN, his mother insisted that she give birth in a stable as the mother of Jesus had done. His family was rich, but Francis lived as a beggar. He said Christ asked true believers to give up everything and follow Him.

Francis gathered followers who all lived in poverty as monks. The order Francis founded still follows his teaching today. The monks who belong to it are called Franciscans. They live very simply, and they care for the sick. They travel all over the world teaching and looking after the poor.

Francis also inspired women to live quiet, holy lives. A rich woman of Assisi named Clare started an order for nuns devoted to God and poverty. When Francis died, his funeral procession stopped at her convent to let Clare say her sad farewell to the gentle monk.

This saint believed the world is good because it is God's creation.

He also believed all creatures were his brothers and his sisters. People saw how happy he was, and stories were told of how nature loved him.

Francis once passed a flock of birds in a field. He called to them, "Praise the Lord, my little sisters." The birds flew to him and listened very quietly as he told them of the love of God. Then they flew off singing with joy.

There is a statue of the saint in Assisi. Ever since it was put up, there have always been two doves living near the statue. When one pair dies, another two birds appear.

OLIVE FESTIVAL

The Italians celebrate the harvest of many of their crops. One of the most traditional celebrations is for the olive, a key ingredient in Italian cooking.

In late summer every year Italian farmers celebrate the coming of the olive harvest. The fruit is not ripe and ready to be picked until early winter.

A good crop is reason to celebrate. The olive has been a vital crop ever since Roman times. The trees grow easily,

DANZA, DANZA, DANZA

Dan - za dan - za dan - za in - tor - no all'u - li - vo,

dan - za, su, dan - za qui sot - to un bel so - le

Tut - ti i bam - bi - ni si dan - no la ma - no,

dan - za, su, dan - za, dan - za con noi.

DANCE, DANCE, DANCE

Dance, dance, dance around
the olive tree,
Come dance, dance under
the shining sun.
All the children, clap their
hands.
Dance, dance, dance with us.

SPAGHETTI WITH GARLIC AND OLIVE OIL

SERVES 4

Salt
12 ounces dried spaghetti
½ cup olive oil
3 garlic cloves, peeled and very finely chopped
3 tbsp finely chopped parsley
1 tsp crushed chilies
Parmesan cheese (optional)

1 Fill a pot with water. Add 3 tbsp salt. Put pot over high heat and bring to a boil.

2 Add spaghetti and stir. Return water to a boil, and cook spaghetti 10 to 12 minutes until just tender when you bite a strand.

3 When spaghetti is almost cooked, heat oil in a deep pot over medium heat. Add garlic, parsley, and chili. Stir and cook 2 minutes. Take pot off heat if garlic starts to look too brown.

4 Pour spaghetti into a large colander in sink. Shake several times to remove any water.

5 Add spaghetti to pot. Stir around so every strand is coated with flavored oil.

6 Serve at once. Sprinkle grated Parmesan cheese over the top, if you like.

even in the poor, thin soil of southern Italy. Olives are used in many different Italian dishes, and the fruit is also pressed to make oil. Harvesting olives is very hard work. Because the fruit bruises, it is harvested by hand. Farmers hang nets beneath the trees and shake them until the olives drop off.

Each year growers bring a sample of last year's oil for tasting. They sprinkle the oil on bread to taste. But an expert can tell if it is good by rubbing the oil onto his palm.

When the harvest is picked and stored, the farmer and his workers relax. At a long table outdoors everyone sits down to a fine meal of pasta, olives, and wine.

FESTA DEI MORTI

The Italians are famous for having very close families. One festival they take very seriously is Festa dei Morti, a day when they pay their respects to any of their relatives who have died.

On November 2, which is known as All Souls' Day, many Italian towns are very quiet. The stores are closed. There is little traffic. But one part of the town is busy: the cemetery.

This is the festival of the dead, when families go to visit the graves of their loved ones. Everyone visits the cemetery to place flowers and wreaths on the graves.

The day is a time for both sorrow and joy.

Tiny images of Jesus adorn candles that will be placed on graves. At dusk the cemeteries twinkle with hundreds and hundreds of tiny flames.

Bread is part of every Italian meal, and by old custom a little loaf was put out in case the dead returned to visit during the Festa dei Morti.

Flowers are placed on the graves in the cemetery. The traditional flowers for the dead are chrysanthemums.

People both miss those who have died and celebrate their lives and the fact that they are now with God.

In past times people used to leave food on the graves as offerings for the dead souls. This does not happen so much today. Instead some people leave food in their kitchen at night. They put small bread buns, candies, and lentils on the table. And they leave all the windows open a crack so that the dead souls can come in.

There are some special foods to be eaten at this time. People bake or buy *pan di mort*, or "bread for the

Sometimes people leave out food for the dead, particularly in southern Italy. Traditionally it includes peas, beans, and lentils or small candies shaped like fruit.

dead." These are sweet cookies made with dried figs.

One particular food that is linked to Festa dei Morti is the lima bean. Not only are beans left out for the dead, there are also cookies baked in the shape of beans. These cookies reflect an old belief from the time of ancient Egypt. The Egyptians thought the spirits of the dead lived inside the beans.

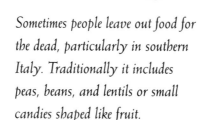

29

STELLA MARIS

Many coastal towns and villages hold fishing festivals to celebrate the riches of the sea. A typical celebration takes place in Taranto in Apulia.

Italy has over 2,000 miles of coastline. Most Italians live relatively close to the sea. For hundreds of years the waters off the coast have been a rich source of food.

Taranto, in the far south, is famous for its shellfish. Fishermen here provide mussels, clams, and oysters for the rest of the country. They are so good that many people eat them raw, fresh from the sea.

Every September the town celebrates with a feast that honors Stella Maris, or the "Star of the Sea." The star is said to protect fishermen at sea. There are barbecues along the shore. Everyone eats grilled and fried shellfish. It is a great chance to enjoy the harvest of the sea.

WORDS TO KNOW

Basilica: A magnificent church building, or the name given to a Roman Catholic church that has been specially privileged by the pope.

Census: A count of all the people in a country, region, or area.

Fast: To go without food deliberately.

Holy Week: The week before Easter when Christians celebrate the last days of Christ's life.

Lent: The 40 days of fasting between Ash Wednesday and Easter.

Medieval: To do with the Middle Ages.

Middle Ages: The period between the fifth and the fifteenth centuries.

Monk: A man who devotes his life to his religion and lives in a monastery.

Patron saint: A saint who watches over a particular group. Nations, towns, and professions all have patron saints.

Peasant: A person who works on the land.

Pilgrim: A person who makes a religious journey, or pilgrimage, to a holy place.

Resurrection: The rising of Christ from the dead on Easter Sunday.

Roman Catholic: A member of the Roman Catholic Church, the largest branch of Christianity. The head of this Church is the pope.

Roman Empire: An ancient empire, which is a country or group of countries ruled by an emperor or an empress. At its height in the second century, the Roman Empire covered much of Europe, North Africa, and the Near East.

Saint: A title given to very holy people by some Christian churches. Saints are important in the Roman Catholic Church.

ACKNOWLEDGMENTS

WITH THANKS TO:

Articles of Faith, Religious Artefacts and Resources for Education, Bury crucifix p13. Catholic Truth Society, London Saint Francis figure p22. Caroline and Isaac Tomiczek knight p17. Tony's Barbershop, Soho, London cart and horses p16-17. Vale Antiques, Elgin Avenue, London ceramic fruit bowl p21.

PHOTOGRAPHS BY:

All photographs by Bruce Mackie.
Cover photograph by Katie Vandyck.

ILLUSTRATIONS BY:

Alison Fleming p4-5, Mountain High Maps ® Copyright © 1993 Digital Wisdom, Inc. p4-5. Tracy Rich p6-7. Alison Fleming p11. Nick Palin(border) p24-5 Susan Moxley (border) p25 Philip Bannister p25.

SET CONTENTS